WHAT WOULD IT TAKE TO MAKE AN ENERGY BLADE?

BY ROBERTA BAXTER

CAPSTONE PRESS
a capstone imprint

Capstone Captivate is published by Capstone Press, an imprint of Capstone.
1710 Roe Crest Drive
North Mankato, Minnesota 56003
www.capstonepub.com

Library of Congress Cataloging-in-Publication Data
Names: Baxter, Roberta, 1952- author.
Title: What would it take to make an energy blade? / by Roberta Baxter.
Description: North Mankato, Minnesota : Capstone Press, 2020. | Series: Sci-fi tech |
    Includes bibliographical references and index. | Audience: Grades 4-6.
Identifiers: LCCN 2019029496 (print) | LCCN 2019029497 (ebook) | ISBN 9781543591170
(hardcover) | ISBN 9781496665973 (paperback) | ISBN 9781543591255 (ebook)
Subjects: LCSH: Stun guns--Juvenile literature. | Torches--Juvenile literature. |
    Laser weapons--Juvenile literature. | Directed-energy weapons--Juvenile literature. |
    Swords--Juvenile literature.
Classification: LCC TK7882.S78 B39 2020 (print) | LCC TK7882.S78 (ebook) | DDC 623.4--dc23
LC record available at https://lccn.loc.gov/2019029496
LC ebook record available at https://lccn.loc.gov/2019029497

Image Credits
Alamy: AF archive, 10; iStockphoto: Devrimb, 5, Marc Dufresne, 28, zegers06, 7; NASA: JSC, 24–25; Newscom: Charles Platiau/Reuters, 8–9; Red Line Editorial: 13; Shutterstock Images: Andrey Eremin, 14, Charles-Edouard Cote, 6, Evgenia Parajanian, 19, Ezume Images, 27, gresei, 22, Master1305, cover, Paul Stringer, 20, Stockr, 23, Yury Stroykin, 16–17
Design Elements: Shutterstock Images

Editorial Credits
Editor: Arnold Ringstad; Designer: Laura Graphenteen

All internet sites appearing in back matter were available and accurate when this book was sent to press.

Printed in the United States of America.
PA99

TABLE OF CONTENTS

WORDS IN BOLD ARE IN THE GLOSSARY.

CHAPTER ONE

SWORDS OF LIGHT

A hero and his enemy face off. They each hold a shiny rod. Suddenly a bright beam of energy grows out of each rod. The beam stops after a few feet. The weapons look like glowing swords. The energy blades hum as they swish through the air. The two fighters attack. Sparks fly as blade strikes blade.

Energy blades are most famous in *Star Wars*. In these movies they are called lightsabers. But energy blades show up in many science-fiction movies, books, and games. Is it possible to build one of these weapons in real life?

Energy blades are popular weapons in science fiction.

Energy blades give off
a bright glow.

CHAPTER TWO

WHAT IS AN ENERGY BLADE?

Energy blades look like swords. But instead of metal, they have blades made of energy. The blades glow with power.

When the blade is turned off, it looks like a flashlight. When the user turns it on, energy shoots out from one or both ends. It forms the glowing blade.

Energy blades have handles that let users safely hold them.

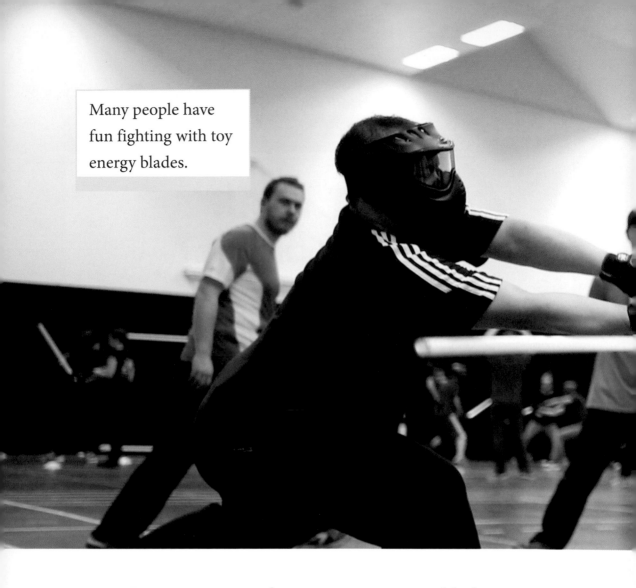

Many people have fun fighting with toy energy blades.

In many science-fiction stories, energy blades are used as weapons. Enemies fight in battles that look like sword fights. The blades spark as they hit each other. The air around them crackles with energy. If a blade hits a person, it can be deadly. The energy can cut a person.

An energy blade is also a tool. It can cut or melt almost anything. In movies people use them to cut through thick steel doors. This kind of blade would be useful in the real world. People could slice through metal objects. They could heat metal to **weld** things together. But is it even possible to make an energy blade?

The *Star Wars* movies have the most famous energy blades in science fiction.

CHAPTER THREE

HOW WOULD AN ENERGY BLADE WORK?

Energy blades in science fiction are often mysterious. They usually do not have real science behind them. Thcy are based in fiction. Scientists have thought about how they could work in the real world. They have a few different ideas.

THE FORCE

In the *Star Wars* movies, the energy blades are powered by a crystal. The crystal uses energy from an invisible energy source called the Force. This source is found everywhere in the galaxy. Special fighters called Jedi can use the Force. They use lightsabers as their weapons.

One idea is to use **lasers**. A laser makes a narrow, focused beam of light. Laser pointers are common toys. More powerful lasers can burn their targets. They can pop balloons or start fires.

But making an energy blade from a laser would be hard. A beam of light from a laser does not stop until it hits something. An energy blade extends only a few feet. The user would need some way to stop the beam. Also, a laser beam is usually invisible. It is only seen when it hits something. Energy blades are bright and visible.

HOW LASERS WORK

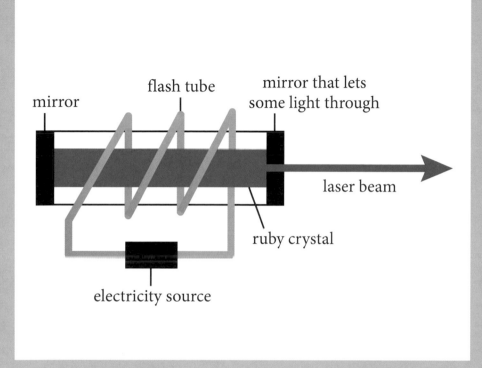

mirror

flash tube

mirror that lets
some light through

laser beam

ruby crystal

electricity source

In a laser, a flash tube sends energy to a ruby crystal. Light bounces around inside the crystal and gets stronger. A mirror in the back reflects light back into the crystal. A mirror on the front mostly reflects light back, but it also lets some out. The light that gets out forms the laser beam.

Plasma-cutting tools are used today to slice through steel.

Another idea is to use **plasma**. When gas has a lot of energy, it becomes a plasma. Plasma is very hot. It can cut through metal. Could we make a blade from a beam of plasma?

One challenge has to do with energy. Creating plasma takes a lot of energy. There is no known way to store enough energy in a small handle.

Making the plasma into a blade shape is another challenge. **Magnetic fields** may help. They could shape the plasma into a long beam. But devices that make strong magnetic fields are large. Scientists don't know how to make them small enough to fit in an energy blade.

FUN FACT

You see plasma at work every day. Neon signs, some light bulbs, and the sun all contain plasma!

Beams of light usually pass through each other.

A third idea uses **photons**. Ordinary light is made up of tiny particles called photons. A beam of light usually passes through another beam of light. But scientists have made a new form of photons. They stick together. They bounce off each other. This is similar to what happens when energy blades crash together.

Making an energy blade with photons would be hard. The new form of photons can only be made at very cold temperatures. Scientists make them in carefully controlled labs.

CHAPTER FOUR

CURRENT TECH

No one has made a real energy blade yet. But one company has made a device that is a little like an energy blade. It is called the TEC Torch. The device is the size of a flashlight. It shoots out a flame that can cut through metal. The torch does not use plasma. Instead it makes a very hot flame.

Inside the device are fuel cartridges. They contain chemicals that mix together. The mixture makes a lot of heat. The device has a **nozzle** at the end. This makes the flame shoot out in a thin, fast beam. The flame cuts through metal quickly. But the cartridges run out of fuel in one or two seconds. The torch is designed for police officers or soldiers. They can use it to cut chains or locks.

FUN FACT

The TEC Torch's flame reaches nearly 5,000 degrees Fahrenheit (2,700 degrees Celsius)!

The TEC Torch would let people quickly slice through metal chains and locks.

Products that look like energy blades are just for show. They are not meant to actually hit things.

Another company makes a product that looks like an energy blade. The company creates powerful handheld lasers. It makes a plastic blade that attaches to a laser. The laser lights up the plastic. It looks like an energy blade from movies.

This handheld laser may be cool to look at. But it doesn't actually work. The blade cannot cut through anything. The company says you should not swing it. The blade is fragile. The plastic could break easily. This blade is just for show.

LASER DANGERS

Handheld lasers do not slice through things like energy blades in movies. But they are still dangerous. Looking at a laser beam can damage the eyes. Pointing it at a person or pet can cause burns. Using them outside is risky too. The beam may shine into the eyes of a driver or pilot. This may cause the driver or pilot to crash.

WHAT TECH IS NEEDED?

An energy blade is not possible with today's technology. What new technologies are needed?

One important thing is a power source. Lasers and plasma need a lot of energy. Today's batteries cannot store that much power in an energy blade handle. An energy blade like the ones in movies would need about 20 **megawatts** of power. That's enough to run more than 10,000 homes! Fitting that much power into a small device is a huge challenge.

Battery technology must improve to make energy blades real.

A real-life energy blade
would take as much energy as
it takes to power a small city.

Forming a blade shape is another major challenge. Magnetic fields can shape plasma. But making magnetic fields takes a lot of energy. This means even more power is needed.

Energy blades in movies can cut through objects. But they can be blocked by other energy blades. This is not how a laser or plasma works. They would simply pass through one another. How could we match the way energy blades work in movies?

One way would be a **ceramic** core. Ceramic is a hard material. It can take a lot of heat without breaking. The plasma could surround the ceramic. The heat would let blades slice through most objects. But two blades would not pass through each other. Scientists would also need to figure out how a long ceramic rod could pop out of a small handle.

The bottom of the space shuttles were covered in ceramic tiles to protect the ships from intense heat.

WHAT COULD THE FUTURE LOOK LIKE?

A real-life energy blade could have many uses. Soldiers could use it as a weapon. The police could use it to break locks or open doors. Construction workers could use it as a tool to cut metal or weld objects together.

The technology behind an energy blade would have other uses too. Small power sources would be very valuable. Normally homes get power from power plants. A home could use these new tiny power sources instead.

Energy blades could
be useful in battles and
for everyday uses.

Energy blades may be popular toys today, but scientists are working to make them into useful tools.

The technology for a real energy blade has not been invented yet. But scientists keep learning more. They are learning more about lasers. They are studying plasma and how to use magnets to shape it. They are learning about photons.

We may not see energy blades like in the movies soon. But studying the technologies behind them could help push science forward. And someday we may end up with a true energy blade. What would you use it for?

GLOSSARY

ceramic (sur-AM-ik)—a hard, heat-resistant material often made of clay

laser (LAY-zur)—a device that creates a beam of tightly focused light

magnetic field (mag-NET-ik FEELD)—the area around something that is acting as a magnet

megawatt (MEG-uh-watt)—an amount of power equal to 1 million watts

nozzle (NAW-zul)—a shaped hole at the end of an object that controls how a gas or liquid comes out of the object

photon (FOE-tawn)—a tiny particle that makes up light

plasma (PLAZ-muh)—what gas becomes when a lot of energy is run through it

weld (WELD)—to heat up metal objects, melt them, and join them together

READ MORE

Adler, David A. *Solids, Liquids, Gases, and Plasma.* New York: Holiday House, 2019.

Hidalgo, Pablo. *Star Wars Lightsabers: A Guide to Weapons of the Force.* Seattle, WA: becker&mayer! kids, 2018.

Spilsbury, Richard, and Louise Spilsbury. *Sources of Light.* Chicago: Heinemann-Raintree, 2016.

INTERNET SITES

How Magnets Work
https://www.ece.neu.edu/fac-ece/nian/mom/work.html

NASA: What Is a Laser?
https://spaceplace.nasa.gov/laser/en/

Star Wars: Lightsaber Crystal
https://www.starwars.com/databank/lightsaber-crystal

INDEX